W9-AXQ-648

SCHOLASTIC

Quick Cloze Passages
for Boosting Comprehension

Grades 4–6

Edited by Karen Baicker

NEW YORK · TORONTO · LONDON · AUCKLAND · SYDNEY
MEXICO CITY · NEW DELHI · HONG KONG · BUENOS AIRES

Teaching Resources

The reproducible pages in this book may be reproduced for classroom use. No part of this publication may be reproduced in whole or in part, or stored in a retrieval system, or transmitted in any form or by any means, electronic, photocopying, recording, or otherwise, without written permission of the publisher. For information regarding permission, write to Scholastic Inc., 557 Broadway, New York, NY 10012.

Cover design by Jason Robinson
Interior design by Kathy Massaro
Interior illustration by Mike Gordon

ISBN 978-0-545-30110-7

Text copyright © 2012 by Scholastic Inc.
Illustrations copyright © 2012 by Scholastic Inc.
Published by Scholastic Inc.
All rights reserved.

9 10   40   19 18 17

Contents

The Passages

Introduction

Welcome to *Quick Cloze Passages for Boosting Comprehension: Grades 4–6.* The cloze-format reading passages in this book are designed to help you teach and reinforce vocabulary and build key reading comprehension and critical thinking skills. Each engaging, fill-in-the-blank passage offers students opportunities to fill in missing words from a companion word list. Because students must interact with the text to fill in the missing words, they become active participants in the reading process.

About the Cloze Passages

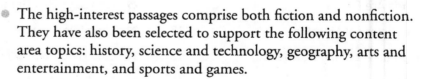

- Each passage appears on a single page, so that it is easy to reproduce and distribute. The passages progress from lower to higher reading levels. On page 6, you'll find a listing of Flesch-Kincaid readability levels for each. Use these grade level scores to match the passages to different students' abilities.

- The high-interest passages comprise both fiction and nonfiction. They have also been selected to support the following content area topics: history, science and technology, geography, arts and entertainment, and sports and games.

- Each word list includes all of the word choices students need to complete the passage, helping them identify vocabulary that might otherwise be beyond their reach. The target words, like the passages, progress from easier to more challenging. These words have been chosen to build reading skills and stretch students' vocabulary with words they are likely to encounter in other contexts.

- To determine the right word for each blank, students practice key reading comprehension skills, such as tapping prior knowledge of the topic and using context clues.

- At the end of each passage, a Think About It question gives students practice in building different reading comprehension skills, such as identifying details, comparing and contrasting, summarizing, and making inferences. The chart at the bottom of page 6 shows the skills targeted in the Think About It question for different passages.

Teaching Tips

- Refer to page 7 to see how the activities in this book align with the Common Core State Standards.

- You can use the activities to assess students' progress and to provide preparation for standardized tests. To monitor students' work, see the answer key on page 48.

Quick Cloze Passages for Boosting Comprehension: Grades 4–6 © 2012 by Scholastic Teaching Resource

Introducing the Cloze Passages

Model for students how to work with the cloze passages by having them follow these steps:

1. Read the title, introduction, and then the passage. Get a feel for what it's about and why it was written. Don't try to fill in any words yet.

2. Reread the entire passage. Think about the kind of word that might fit each blank. Look at the other words in the sentence for clues about the word that is missing.

3. Read through the word list. Look for the words that are closest in meaning to the words you're already considering.

4. When you find a match, write it in the blank.

5. When you've completed the passage, read it through with your answers in place to make sure it makes sense.

Ways to Use the Cloze Passages

The cloze passage activities are flexible and easy to use in a variety of ways:

*   **Small Group:** Distribute copies of the same passage to each member of a small group (4–5 students). Have students read and fill in the blanks. Then have them trade passages to check each other's work. One student can read the completed passage aloud.

*   **Individual Desk Work While Conferencing:** Distribute a passage to each student to work on while you conference with individual students about their cloze passages or about other academic subjects.

*   **Homework:** Send copies of passages home for vocabulary reinforcement and reading practice, and for students to complete with their families as a school-home connection.

Do More!

*   Distribute the cloze passages without the word list. Let students try to come up with their own vocabulary choices and read their passages aloud to the class.

*   Once students have gotten the hang of cloze passages, you can also create your own using other classroom materials, such as picture books, science texts, and social studies passages. Photocopy the passage once and use correction fluid to create blank spaces. Include a word list of the missing words in alphabetical order.

Readability Levels of the Passages

The chart below indicates the Flesch-Kincaid reading level for each of the passages. You can use these grade-level scores to determine which passages are appropriate for the abilities of different students.

1	**Written by Anonymous**	RL 1.5		21	**The Bear Facts**	RL 5.2
2	**The Sun and the Wind**	RL 2.5		22	**Rainforest Medicines**	RL 5.3
3	**Wanda and Tina**	RL 3.1		23	**We All Scream for Ice Cream!**	RL 5.3
4	**The Gift**	RL 3.6		24	**Baseball Is a Hit in Japan**	RL 5.4
5	**Three Friends**	RL 3.7		25	**She Climbed to the Top**	RL 5.6
6	**How Coyote Won His Dinner**	RL 3.8		26	**The Panama Canal**	RL 5.6
7	**Marly and the Kite**	RL 3.9		27	**Helpful Houseplants**	RL 5.6
8	**Rocket Man**	RL 4.1		28	**Faithfully Ours**	RL 5.7
9	**Yo-Yos Are Forever**	RL 4.2		29	**Who Says Ball Games Are for the Birds?**	RL 5.8
10	**The History of Marbles**	RL 4.2		30	**Long Life**	RL 5.9
11	**One Cool-Looking Cowhand**	RL 4.2		31	**Kids Help Pass Safety Laws**	RL 6.3
12	**Malik and Me**	RL 4.2		32	**The Perfect Pet**	RL 6.4
13	**Color Me Happy!**	RL 4.3		33	**Presidential Pets**	RL 6.5
14	**Frozen Treat**	RL 4.6		34	**Knuckle Cracking**	RL 6.6
15	**Giving TV the Boot**	RL 4.6		35	**Why Penguins Wear Tuxedos**	RL 6.7
16	**The Midas Touch**	RL 4.7		36	**Endurance**	RL 6.9
17	**Smokejumpers**	RL 4.7		37	**Here Comes the…Maildog?**	RL 7.1
18	**Fooled You!**	RL 4.7		38	**Old Bones**	RL 7.2
19	**The King's Things**	RL 4.8		39	**What's the Word?**	RL 7.2
20	**The *Titanic***	RL 5.0		40	**Endangered Animals**	RL 7.4

Building Comprehension Skills

The chart below shows the reading comprehension skill targeted in the Think About It question for different passages.

Skill	Passage #
Analyze Character	5, 29
Recognize Cause & Effect	2, 13, 28, 30, 31, 35
Compare & Contrast	1, 12, 21, 24
Distinguish Between Fact & Opinion	8, 20, 23, 32, 34

Skill	Passage #
Identify Details	9, 22, 37, 40
Make Inferences	5, 16, 19, 33, 38, 39
Identify Problem & Solution	3, 4, 15, 25, 26
Understanding Sequence	6, 7, 10, 17, 18, 36
Summarize	11, 14, 27

Quick Cloze Passages for Boosting Comprehension: Grades 4–6 © 2012 by Scholastic Teaching Resources

Meeting the Common Core State Standards

The cloze passage activities and companion reading comprehension questions in this book will help you meet your specific state reading and language arts standards as well as those recommended by the Common Core State Standards Initiative (CCSSI). These materials address the following standards for students in grades 4-6. For more information, visit the CCSSI Web site: www.corestandards.org.

Reading Standards for Literature

Key Ideas and Details

* RL.4.1, RL.5.1, RL.6.2: Refer to details in a text when explaining what the text says explicitly and when drawing inferences from the text.

* RL.4.2, RL.5.2, RL.6.2: Determine a theme of a story from details in the text; summarize the text.

* RL.4.3, RL.5.3: Describe a character, setting or event in a story, drawing on specific details in the text.

Range of Reading and Level of Text Complexity

* RL.4.10, RL.5.10: By the end of the year, read and comprehend literature in the grades 4–5 text complexity band proficiently, with scaffolding as needed (grade 4); at the high end of the grades 4–5 text complexity band independently and proficiently (grade 5).

* RL.6.10: By the end of the year, read and comprehend literature in the grades 6–8 text complexity band proficiently, with scaffolding as needed.

Craft and Structure

* RL.4.4, RL.5.4, RL.6.4: Determine the meaning of words and phrases as they are used in a text.

Reading Standards for Informational Text

Key Ideas and Details

* RI.4.1, RI.5.1, RI.6.1: Refer to details and examples in a text when explaining what the text says explicitly and when drawing inferences from the text.

* RI.4.2, RI.6.2: Determine main idea of a text and explain how it is supported by key details; summarize the text.

* RI.4.3: Explain events, procedures, ideas, or concepts in a historical, scientific, or technical text, including what happened and why, based on specific information in the text.

Craft and Structure

* RI.4.4, RI.5.4, RI.6.4: Determine the meaning of general academic and domain-specific words or phrases in a text.

* RI.4.5, RI.5.5: Describe the overall structure (e.g., chronology, comparison, cause/effect, problem/ solution) of events or information in a text or part of a text.

Range of Reading and Level of Text Complexity

* RI.4.10, RI.5.10: By the end of year, read and comprehend informational texts in the grades 4-5 text complexity band proficiently, with scaffolding as needed (grade 4); at the high end of the grades 4-5 text complexity band independently and proficiently (grade 5).

* RI.6.10: By the end of the year, read and comprehend literary nonfiction in the grades 6–8 text complexity band proficiently, with scaffolding as needed.

Reading Standards: Foundational Skills

* RF.4.4, RF.5.4: Read with sufficient accuracy and fluency to support comprehension.

* RF.4.4a, RF.5.4a: Read on-level text with purpose and understanding.

* RF.4.4c, RF.5.4c: Use context to confirm or self-correct word recognition and understanding, rereading as necessary.

Language Standards

Vocabulary Acquisition and Use

* L.4, L.5, L.6: Determine or clarify the meaning of unknown and multiple-meaning words and phrases, choosing flexibly from a range of strategies.

* L.4.4a, L.5.4a, L.6.4a: Use context as a clue to the meaning of a word or phrase.

* L.4.5, L.5.5, L.6.5: Demonstrate understanding of figurative language, word relationships, and nuances in word meanings.

Name _____ Date _____

Written by Anonymous

The poems that follow were signed "Anonymous," meaning the author is unknown. Enjoy the poetry as you fill in the blanks.

The Joke

The joke you told isn't funny one bit.

It's _____ and dull, wholly lacking in wit.

It's so old and stale; it's beginning to smell!

Besides, it's the one I was going to tell.

—Anonymous

Word List

considering

distracted

flaw

imprisoned

pointless

The Puzzled Centipede

A centipede was happy quite

Until a frog in fun

Said, "Pray, which leg comes after which?"

This raised her mind to such a pitch,

She lay _____ in the ditch

_____ how to run.

—Anonymous

A Fly and a Flea in a Flue

A fly and a flea in a flue

Were _____, so what could they do?

Said the fly, "Let us flee!"

"Let us fly!" said the flea,

And they flew through a _____ in the flue.

—Anonymous

Think About It!

How are these poems alike? How are they different?

Name _____ Date _____

The Sun and the Wind

Wind can be very powerful, and so can the sun. According to a legend, the two once had an argument about who was stronger. Fill in the blanks in this fable to see who won.

One day the sun and the wind had an argument. The wind

_____ that he was stronger than the sun.

"Wrong," replied the sun. "I am stronger than you."

As they were _____, a woman came

down the road, wearing a heavy woolen coat.

"Here's how we can decide who is stronger," shouted the wind.

"See that woman. Let's see which of us can remove her coat."

"Good idea," the sun replied. "You go first." So the wind started to blow.

He blew and blew, as hard as he could. Trees swayed almost to the ground, but

the woman only _____ her coat more tightly around

her.

Now the sun began to shine. She shone down on the woman, until the

woman grew warm and _____ her coat. The sun kept

on shining. Soon, the woman removed her coat and laid it over her arm.

"Alas, you win," said the wind to the sun. "Your

_____ has succeeded where my rudeness failed."

Word List

claimed

disagreeing

gentleness

unbuttoned

wrapped

Think About It! How did the sun get the woman to remove her coat?

Name _____ Date _____

Wanda and Tina

What do you do if your best friend suddenly stops talking to you? Fill in the blanks in this story to see what one girl does in that situation.

Wanda and Tina had been best friends for years. That's why Wanda was so _____ one day when Tina wouldn't talk to her. She had saved Tina a seat in the _____, but when Tina came in she went off and sat by herself.

Wanda didn't know what was wrong. Could Tina be mad at her? She thought about what she had done and said _____. Was Tina upset because Wanda had done better on the history test? No, Tina was _____ happy that Wanda did well at school.

Wanda decided to find out what was the matter. She walked over to where Tina was sitting. "Tina," she said softly, "Is something wrong?"

Tina looked up, _____ perplexed. Then she realized who it was. "Oh, hi, Wanda," she said. "Yes, something is wrong. My cat Zorro died yesterday. I've been really sad. Thanks for asking. You're a true friend." Wanda sat down next to her friend and gave her a big hug.

Word List

astonished
genuinely
lunchroom
momentarily
recently

Think About It!

How did Wanda solve the problem she was having with Tina?

Name _____ Date _____

The Gift

Sometimes it's hard to give the perfect gift, especially when you don't have much money to spend. Fill in the blanks to see how one boy solves this problem.

Sam got an email _____ from Rosa to her birthday party. Although, this would normally have made him happy, his father had recently lost his job. Sam only had a few dollars, and it wasn't a good time to ask his parents for help.

Sam went to work at the library. As he left, he saw a sign for a book sale. Two books _____ his attention. The first was a cookbook of Puerto Rican foods. The second was about women explorers. Both seemed perfect for Rosa—but would used books be too _____?

Well, it was better than no gift at all! The next day, he wrapped them and headed to her party. Everyone had a great time, but Sam was still _____ about his gift.

When he got home, he found an email from Rosa saying: *Of all the gifts I _____ today, yours was the nicest. How did you know just what I would love? Thank you for being such a wonderful friend!*

Word List

anxious
captured
invitation
tacky
received

Think About It!

What was Sam's problem, and how did he solve it?

Name _____   Date _____

Three Friends

How can a tiny, lonely turtle make friends with two big animals? Fill in the blanks in this story to find out.

A lonely Turtle wanted some new friends. So Turtle went to

his _____, Elephant, who was happily

eating grass. Turtle said, "Elephant, let's have a tug-of war in the

field. If I can stay on my feet, will you be my friend?"

    Elephant _____ and agreed.

Then Turtle went through the forest to Hippopotamus, who

was floating in the river. Turtle asked the same question. Hippo

laughed, too. "All right, Turtle. If you win, we'll be friends."

    So Turtle got some _____ and a long,

strong rope. He gave one end of the rope to Elephant and said, "Hold this

rope. Don't pull until you hear me whistle." Then Turtle took the other

end of the rope through the forest to Hippo and told him the same thing.

    When Turtle whistled, Elephant and Hippo pulled and pulled and

huffed and puffed. After a while, Turtle cut the rope. Elephant and Hippo

both _____ down with a thud. Turtle's plan

was a _____. Now Elephant, Hippo, and

Turtle are all friends.

Word List

- chuckled
- neighbor
- scissors
- success
- tumbled

Think About It!

What words would you use to describe Turtle?

Name _____ Date _____

How Coyote Won His Dinner

Fill in the blanks in this fable to find out how Coyote won dinner for the rest of his life.

At least three times a week, Coyote sneaked into Mr. Hank's ranch and stole chickens or eggs.

"Coyote," Mr. Hank said one day, "I'll make you a deal. If you can steal my clothes tonight, I'll give you three chickens a week, forever. If I catch you, promise never to steal from me again."

"Okay," said Coyote, "it's a deal."

That night, Mr. Hank told Mrs. Hank about the deal, putting his clothes on a table in the bedroom. He sat on one side of the table in his _____, and she sat on the other. Shortly, Mr. Hank heard his horses running _____ outside. He asked Mrs. Hank to _____ the clothes while he went to _____.

Now Coyote went to the window and called in, "You'd better hand me those clothes, dear. That _____ might steal them while I'm gone."

Mrs. Hank, thinking it was her husband, handed the clothes out the window. And that is how Coyote earned his dinner for the rest of his life.

Word List

guard
investigate
nightshirt
thief
wildly

Think About It!

What happened just before Mr. Hanks left the bedroom?

Name _____ Date _____

Marly and the Kite

Have you ever flown a kite? Fill in the blanks in this story to read about one girl who makes her own.

Marly's class was studying China. Her teacher told them that kites were invented in China more than 2,000 years ago. Then she gave them an unusual homework _____. "The Chinese make kites that represent something important to them. Each of you should make a kite that _____ something important to you.

"I don't know how to make a kite," Marly _____ on the way home. She decided to ask her dad for help.

"What do you think of when you see a kite?" her dad asked.

Marly thought for a moment and answered, "Eagles."

Marly's dad agreed that would make an _____ design. They used balsa wood to make a cross. Marly painted a golden eagle on a white sheet. They stretched it over the rods, making a diamond-shape. Then they tied a long tail to the bottom.

Next, they took the kite to the park and tested it. Marly jerked the string and made the kite _____, so that the kite dived to the earth and flew back up again.

"Wow!" she cried proudly. "This eagle soars!"

Word List

assignment
excellent
grumbled
signifies
swoop

Think About It! What happened after Marly and her dad finished making her kite?

Name _____ Date _____

Rocket Man

What's it like to be in outer space? Fill in the blanks in this interview with former astronaut Tom Jones for some inside information.

Question: When did you decide to become an astronaut?

Tom Jones: When I was 10. It was 1965, and U.S. astronauts were practicing for the first trips to the moon.

Question: What does it feel like when you blast off?

Tom Jones: First there's a rumble as the engines fire up. Then there's a huge jolt. The _____ against your chest builds. It feels like a 700-pound _____ is sitting on your chest.

Question: What does it feel like to be _____?

Tom Jones: It's very _____, like you're floating underwater. With a touch of your finger, you can push off and glide wherever you want.

Question: What's cool about being in space?

Tom Jones: The _____ view of Earth. You can float over to the window and catch glimpses of oceans, snow-covered forests, and deserts.

Word List

gorilla
peaceful
pressure
vivid
weightless

Think About It!

Name one fact and one opinion in the interview.

Name _____ Date _____

Yo-Yos Are Forever

People never seem to tire of yo-yos. Fill in the blanks in this article to find out why people of all ages continue to like this toy.

Why do people find yo-yos so _____?
For one thing, they're fun. Another reason is that toy makers keep
making better yo-yos.

Years ago, yo-yos were made of wood. Wooden parts can wear
out quickly. Toy makers tried new ideas. Some began using plastic
instead of wood. Plastic parts last longer.

Toy makers also search for the ideal kind of string. It has to let
the yo-yo glide up and down easily, and needs to be thin. Yet it must
be _____, so it does not break easily.

Toy makers are also making new yo-yos that look very
_____. Some have colored
_____ painted on the outside. Others look
like butterflies as they spin. Some light up and play music. Some have
cloth _____ that make them look like round,
furry animals. These yo-yos make it even more fun to do cool tricks, such
as "walking the dog," "rocking the cradle," and going "around the world."

Word List

appealing
coverings
designs
durable
unusual

Think About It!

What are some ways that toy makers have changed yo-yos?

The History of Marbles

Fill in the blanks in this article to learn about a common, everyday game with a long history.

Grab a bag with an _____ of those little colored balls. They may be striped or speckled, cloudy or clear. They are made of clay, glass, or plastic, and can glitter like a bag of _____.

Marbles made of stone and clay have been found in ancient tombs in Egypt. Artwork from ancient Rome shows children playing games with marbles. The Romans brought the game to England. Then the English brought it to America, where George Washington and Thomas Jefferson played marbles. Abraham Lincoln was an _____ player.

To set up a game of marbles, draw a large circle on smooth ground. Form an "X" using 13 marbles inside the circle. This is your _____. Players gather at the circle's edge. To play, hold a marble between your index finger and thumb. A small _____ will _____ it forward. If you hit another marble, you will send it flying. The first player to knock seven marbles out of the circle wins the game.

Word List

assortment
expert
flick
jewels
propel
target

Think About It!

What is the first thing you do when you play the game of marbles?

Quick Cloze Passages for Boosting Comprehension: Grades 4–6 © 2012 by Scholastic Teaching Resources

Name _____ Date _____

One Cool-Looking Cowhand

The cowhands of the Old West were pretty cool characters. Fill in the blanks in this article to find out what a cowhand wore.

Cowhands, another name for cowboys and cowgirls, were important workers in the Old West. They drove herds of cattle across the plains to railroad stations, where they were loaded on trains and taken to market. What did they wear, and why?

Cowhands always wore big hats to keep out the dirt and shade them from the sun. Cowhands also used their hats to carry water. They tapped their hats to say hello and waved them to _____ happiness.

They wore _____ to keep dust out of their mouths. These cloths also came in handy as scarves and _____.

Cowhands wore long-sleeved shirts, vests, and jeans. Over their jeans, cowhands wore leather _____ to protect their jeans from the rough country _____.

On their feet, cowhands wore tall boots, protecting their feet and shins. The boots were high enough to keep out dust, dirt, stones, and water. There were spurs on the backs of the boots. Cowhands used spurs to prod their horses to "Get a move on!"

Word List

bandages
bandannas
brush
chaps
signal

Think About It!

What pieces of clothing did cowhands wear, and why did they wear them?

Quick Close Passages for Boosting Comprehension: Grades 4–5 © 2012 by Scholastic Teaching Resources

Name _____ Date _____

Malik and Me

Have you ever had someone who gets under your skin? Fill in the blanks in this story to see what happens when one girl decides to face the problem head-on.

There are four things you need to know about Malik Jones.
1. He's in my homeroom. 2. He plays baseball. 3. He gets good grades. 4. He's the most annoying person who ever lived.

I mean, why would a person _____ stare at me, or talk about my hair, unless it was to _____ me? No matter where I am, Malik is _____ to walk by and make some supposedly funny comment. Everyone else thinks it's amusing, but I find it highly annoying.

So the other day, I finally _____ him. "Malik Jones," I said. "What makes you think you can always talk about my hair?" He looked _____ for a minute. "Well," he finally said, "I like your hair. That's why I'm always talking about it. I think it's beautiful."

Did I mention that Malik Jones is one of the nicest guys who ever lived?

Word List

confronted
continually
guaranteed
irritate
startled

Think About It!

Compare and contrast the narrator's view of Malik at the beginning of the story and at the end.

Name _____   Date _____

Color Me Happy!

What color helps students get higher test scores? Fill in the blanks in the article to find out.

Do you like blue candy? Most people _____ blue food, because most foods are not _____ blue. Our brains just don't connect the color blue with tasty food. Try this: Replace the bulb in your refrigerator with a blue bulb. When you look at blue milk and eggs, you'll probably stop feeling hungry!

Word List

avoid

influences

naturally

nervous

significantly

surrounding

However, blue has a different effect as a room color. In one classroom that had dark blue walls, students got _____ higher test scores. In dark blue gyms, weight lifters lifted heavier weights. How can this effect be explained?

Scientists think that color may affect your mood. And the way you feel _____ the way you behave.

In a dark blue room, students will feel strong and smart. If the walls are pale blue, students may not pay attention. Yellow walls make students _____ —and jumpy students don't do well on tests!

So, if you want to feel happy, strong, and smart, think about the colors _____ you. Changing colors can change your mood.

Think About It!

What are some of the effects that color has on people's mood and behavior?

Frozen Treat

On a scorching hot day, there's nothing better than cooling off with an icy treat. Fill in the blanks to learn about how one kid invented a treat that sold millions.

The next time you cool off with an ice-cold Popsicle®, you can thank Frank Epperson. He was just 11 years old when he came up with his _____ frozen treat. Here is what happened.

In 1905, young Frank mixed together some

_____ soda pop with water

to drink. He left the cup on the back porch

_____ with the stirring stick still in it.

When Frank went out to the porch the next morning, he found a stick of frozen soda water. He brought it to school that day. Soon, he was selling his _____ to friends.

The rest, as they say, is history. When Frank grew up, he

_____ his invention and named it the

Popsicle®. By 1928, more than 60 million Popsicles® had been sold.

Word List

creation
famous
overnight
patented
powdered

Think About It!   How was the Popsicle® invented?

Name _____ Date _____

Giving TV the Boot

Are you an average American kid? If so, you watch as much as 28 hours of TV a week. Imagine all of the things you could do with that time! Fill in the blanks to learn about what two families do with that extra time.

The Weiskopfs

Saying "no" to TV isn't new for Ethan and Matthew Weiskopf. Every

year, they _____ in TV-Turnoff week.

"Sometime I get bored and miss TV," says Ethan. "But most of

the time, I think it's fun."

Ethan's older brother Matthew agrees with him. He

_____ a new hobby, building models,

during his first week without TV. "When kids turn off the TV, they

get to use their other _____," says Matthew.

The Oberlins

The Oberlins turned off TV for more than a week—they turned it off for good! But

life isn't quiet, nor is it dull. It's filled with noise from the family's dog, pony, goat, cats,

hamsters, and parakeets, and busy with lots of _____, too.

"Without TV, kids have to create their own fun," says their mom. Monica

roller blades and reads...at the same time! She calls it "roller reading." Bonnie

does _____, plays guitar, and paints. There's plenty of

entertainment at the Oberlin house!

Word List

- abilities
- activities
- discovered
- gymnastics
- participate

Think About It! What is the problem described in the article? What are some solutions people came up with to survive without TV?

Name _____ Date _____

The Midas Touch

Have you ever wished that everything you touched turned to gold? Fill in the blanks in this story to find out what might happen if that wish came true.

Many years ago in Greece, there lived a king named Midas. He wished for the power to turn things to gold simply by touching them. Since Midas was a good king, a god named Dionysus _____ his wish. Shouting with joy, Midas ran through his _____ palace, touching everything. And everything he owned became gold. He was rich beyond his wildest dreams.

At dinnertime, King Midas reached for some bread, and the bread turned to gold. He tried to sip some water, and his lips turned the water to gold. King Midas realized that he would soon die of hunger or thirst. Weeping gold tears, he went to the god Dionysus and begged the god to remove the golden touch.

"You have been greedy and _____,"

_____ Dionysus. But he took

_____ on Midas, and sent the king to a special river to wash his hands. Midas did so, and the golden touch was washed away.

Word List

foolish

granted

pity

scolded

vast

Think About It!

What is the lesson the story is trying to teach?

Name _____ Date _____

Smokejumpers

What do smokejumpers do? Fill in the blanks in this article to find out.

A wildfire is spreading in the Montana wilderness. A fire management officer has to decide—and quickly: should she put the fire out or let it burn? Since the forest is so _____, she doesn't want to take any chances that it will spread too far. Time to call in the smokejumpers.

The smokejumpers _____ down from airplanes to try to control wildfires. Their routine begins with digging a fire line to clear a wide path around the fire. If that doesn't work, they change plans. They try to _____ the fire to the forest floor by clearing away low-hanging branches. Flames can climb these branches and speed along _____.

Next, smokejumpers dig through the burned area with special axes and hoes. They dig up cool dirt, trying to _____ the fire.

Their final task is to crawl through the area and feel the ground to make sure it isn't hot. Fires that _____ to be out can sometimes start again.

Word List

- arid
- appear
- confine
- overhead
- parachute
- smother

Think About It!

What sequence do smokejumpers follow to contain a wildfire?

Name _____ Date _____

Fooled You!

April Fools! Has anyone ever pulled a prank on you on this national day of trickery? Fill in the blanks to read one story about an April Fools' prank.

Maria decided to have a Prank Party on April Fools' Day. She invited her best friends to come over that afternoon. She and her mom made some tasty "treats" for the party. They made fried-egg _____. These sweet treats looked like a fried egg in a bowl but were really made from vanilla ice cream topped with _____ fluff and a round blob of yellow pudding.

Next on the menu was "pizza." First, Maria and her mom stirred strawberry and _____ jam together. Then they spread it on a _____, being careful not to go to the edges. They melted white chocolate chips and spread that on the "sauce" for "cheese." Then they cut up licorice sticks to _____ black olives and a fruit roll to look like green peppers.

Her friends loved the tasty pranks. But who knows what she'll do next year!

Word List

apricot
marshmallow
resemble
sundaes
tortilla

Think About It!

What were the steps in making the prank pizza?

Name _____ Date _____

The King's Things

When King Tut of Egypt died, what do you think the ancient Egyptians placed in his tomb? Fill in the blanks in the article to find out.

King Tut, known as the "boy king," died when he was only 16. Although he didn't live long, his tomb tells us that he did live well. Ancient Egyptians believed there was life after death. When Tut died, they packed enough items in his tomb to last him many lifetimes! Take a look at the list of what they packed:

Word List

boomerangs
dazzling
entertainment
fashionable
toiletries

- _____ gold jewelry

- Plenty of food, including raisins, dates, goat, duck, beef, bread, garlic, fruit, and honey

- _____, including a shaving kit and eye make-up

- Hunting tools, such as _____, bows, arrows, knives, and armor

- A trumpet

- Three thrones and six beds

- _____ clothes, including sandals, shirts, caps, gloves, and more

- _____ items, such as game boards, model boats, and a pen with ink

Think About It!   What do the items buried in King Tut's tomb show you about his life?

Name _____ Date _____

The *Titanic*

The *Titanic* was a mighty ship that came to a terrible end. Fill in the blanks to read more about this tragic disaster at sea.

The year is 1912. The day is April 10. The *Titanic* sets sail from England. The _____ ship is three football fields long. Eleven stories high, it is the largest moving object ever built. The ship has elegant restaurants, a swimming pool, and indoor gardens. Some of the world's richest people stroll through its fine rooms. No one seeing it at this moment would _____ that tragedy lies ahead.

It is the ship's first _____. This floating palace is bound for New York City. The crew intends to set a record getting there. The *Titanic* is the most powerful ship on the sea, brags its builder. There is nothing to fear. Let other ships' crews worry about iceberg warnings. Other ships aren't the *Titanic*. The *Titanic* is _____.

Sadly, pride goes before the fall. Around midnight on April 14, 1912, a massive iceberg rips open the mighty ship's steel _____. Tons of water gush in. For the *Titanic*, the end has come.

Word List

- enormous
- hull
- suspect
- unsinkable
- voyage

Think About It!

Name one fact and one opinion in the article.

Name _____ Date _____

The Bear Facts

You probably know at least two things about bears: They're big and they can be scary. Fill in the blanks to learn more about two different kinds of bears.

Although black bears and polar bears are different in many

ways, they also have a lot in common. Their body shape is

_____, and they both have thick coats

of fur. _____ bear cubs of all kinds

are very tiny and stay with their mother for a year or more.

A major difference between black bears and polar bears

is their size. A full-grown black bear can be four to five feet long

and weigh 150 to 400 pounds. The huge polar bear, at six to eight feet long,

can weigh up to 1,500 pounds! Black bears eat mostly green plants, berries,

nuts, ants, and small animals such as _____.

The _____ food of polar bears is seals, although

they also eat birds' eggs and berries.

Black bears have black or dark brown fur. Polar bears have fur that

is yellowish-white. What's another way the two types of bears differ?

Black bears _____ during the winter, while

polar bears remain active.

Word List

chief

hibernate

newborn

rodents

similar

Think About It! How are the black bear and the polar bear alike and different?

Rainforest Medicines

Fill in the blanks to find out about medicines that come from the rainforest.

A young boy is crying because his ear hurts. A man comes out of the forest carrying some juice from a white fungus plant. Carefully, he drips the _____ into the boy's ear. In some rainforest villages of South America, that's how earaches are cured!

Rainforest doctors, called shamans, use many kinds of plants as medicine. They make tea from one type of red vine. It cures stomachaches. Yellow flowers from another plant are used to treat snakebites.

Today, scientists from all over the world want to learn what these shamans know about plant medicines. They are racing to find the secrets of the rainforest before the forests are cleared and the plants disappear for good.

The scientists spend long hours _____ through the _____ jungle with the _____ shamans. The shamans show them which plants can be used as cures.

One U.S. company has already developed a new medicine. It comes from a plant found in Ecuador. This medicine may be used to cure lung _____ in kids.

Word List

infections
liquid
local
steamy
trudging

Think About It!

What are some ways that rainforest plants are used as medicines?

Name _____ Date _____

We All Scream for Ice Cream!

Do most of your friends like ice cream? Chances are they do—Americans are big ice cream lovers. Fill in the blanks to find some interesting facts and figures about just how much we love ice cream.

People in the United States love their ice cream. The average American eats about 47 pints each year. That's almost two hundred scoops of the frozen stuff! There's no _____ about it. We're the biggest ice cream eaters in the world! Who's next? Believe it or not, New Zealand. New Zealanders _____ about 40 pints a year. Australians are in third place at about 32 pints each.

You might _____ that Canadians would be big ice cream eaters. After all, Canada is right next to the United States. The average Canadian, however, only eats about 27 pints. Maybe it's just too cold in Canada to eat that much ice cream.

The top-selling flavor is _____. Some call it boring, but people seem to eat it up. Believe it or not, chocolate is only the fifth favorite flavor. It trails fruit flavors, nut flavors, and candy-mix flavors in _____.

Word List

consume
doubt
expect
popularity
vanilla

Think About It! The article implies that it's too cold to eat ice cream in Canada. Is that a fact or an opinion?

Baseball Is a Hit in Japan

How is baseball in Japan like baseball in the United States? Fill in the blanks in this article to find out.

The October air is crisp and cool. Leaves are on the ground. Inside the ballpark, fans are packed into the stands, watching a baseball game. Sounds like the World Series is under way, right?

Wrong! This game is being played in Japan as part of the Japan Series. That's the Japanese _____ of the World Series.

The Japanese have been playing baseball ever since Americans taught them the game in the 1870s. They have had _____ baseball leagues since 1935. Millions of Japanese _____ ball games every year. When they aren't watching baseball, many fans play the game. Among kids, baseball is Japan's most _____ sport.

Baseball is played by the same basic rules as in the United States. It's a little different, though. In Japan, games can end in a tie, unlike in the United States. And in Japan, fans must return foul balls. Like American fans, however, they get to keep balls hit in homeruns. And in both the U.S. and Japan, most fans _____ their home team.

Word List

attend
prevalent
professional
support
version

Think About It!

What are some of the differences between Japanese and American baseball?

31

Name _____ Date _____

She Climbed to the Top

Read this story to find out about the youngest person to climb Denali, the highest mountain in North America. Use the word list to fill in the blanks.

The wind was _____. Twelve-year-old Merrick Johnston, her mom, and a guide had to take cover— but where? They were more than 14,000 feet up on Denali, America's highest mountain. There was nowhere to go but down into the snow. The group dug a deep snow cave to protect themselves. They waited inside for five days until the storm blew over. Then they continued their record-breaking climb.

Merrick's trip took 26 days. Each person in the group carried a backpack full of food and other _____. The _____ dipped to 30 degrees below zero. The team had to cross dangerous ice _____ and climb icy slopes.

After more than three weeks of climbing, Merrick's group reached the top. Merrick became the youngest person ever to reach the top of the 20,320-foot-high _____ in Alaska.

"We were in the clouds most of the time. But right when we reached the top, we were above the clouds," Merrick recalled.

Word List

- canyons
- howling
- summit
- supplies
- temperatures

Think About It!

How did the climbers handle the challenges of the snowstorm?

Name _____ Date _____

The Panama Canal

In the early 1800s, it used to take a ship several months to sail from New York to California. Fill in the blanks in the article below to find out how a canal was built to solve that problem.

In the 1800s, a ship traveling from New York to California had

to go around the southern tip of South America before sailing

_____ to California. The trip took

several months! A faster route was needed, and Panama offered

that _____.

The Panama Canal is only about 50 miles long. But it took

ten years to build. Workers had to dig all across Panama. They

_____ away tons of dirt. It was not

easy to dig through jungles, hills, and swamps. Insects were a big problem.

Some spread yellow fever and other _____.

To kill the insects, workers _____ swamps and

cleared brush. It was a hard job, but it worked! In 1914, workers finished the

canal—a 7,000-mile _____ for ships!

Word List

diseases
drained
hauled
northward
possibility
shortcut

Think About It!

How was the problem of the very long ocean trip from
New York to California solved?

Name _____ Date _____

Helpful Houseplants

They sit on a desk or table and look pretty. You need to remember to water them. But what are houseplants actually good for? Fill in the blanks to find out.

Scientists say houseplants do more than

_____ homes and offices. They can

also improve the _____ of the air

we breathe. Buildings today are often airtight and have plenty

of _____. This makes them energy-

efficient, but it also makes it hard for fresh air to enter.

Many houseplants can "clean" the stale air trapped inside

buildings. Plant leaves take in the carbon dioxide gas from the air.

In return, they give out clean _____.

Plants also take other dangerous gases from the air. For instance, a

type of daisy takes in benzene, a _____

found in gasoline. Spider plants take in carbon monoxide. So why

not keep a lot of houseplants around? They just might help you

breathe easier.

Word List

chemical

decorate

insulation

oxygen

quality

Think About It!

What are some benefits of houseplants?

Name _____ Date _____

Faithfully Ours

Fill in the blanks in this article to learn about the world's most famous geyser.

Word List

performance
reliability
schedule
spectacle
unpredictable

Whoosh! A stream of water shoots into the sky, spraying visitors with mist. The _____ continues for a few seconds more and then is gone. Cheers burst from the crowd. Old Faithful did it again, right on _____.

As geysers go, Old Faithful in Wyoming's Yellowstone National Park is probably the world's most famous. Geysers are hot springs that shoot water into the air.

The trouble with most geysers is that no one knows when they will decide to spout off. They're an _____ lot. One geyser in New Zealand hasn't been active since 1917. Another geyser, called Giant, sometimes spouts once a week, and other times waits for months.

Old Faithful, however, lives up to its name. For the past 32 years, it hasn't skipped a single _____. About every 76 minutes or so, it shoots its water stream around 150 feet into the air. That kind of _____ draws over three million people to see it every year.

Think About It! How has the geyser called Old Faithful earned its name?

Name _____ Date _____

Who Says Ball Games Are for the Birds?

What do ball games and birds have in common? More than you think! Fill in the blanks in this article to find out.

The Trinity College Bantams were proud of their name. Bantams are a type of rooster, which suited the _____ spirit of this basketball team. One day in 1954, the Trinity Bantams were set to battle Yale's team.

The Trinity fans hatched a "fowl" plan to support their players. When the Bantams scored their first basket, their fans gently _____ dozens of live chickens onto the court! The chickens raced wildly around the floor. The game had to be _____ until all the birds were collected.

Another bird-brained _____ involved Casey Stengel. He played baseball with the Brooklyn Dodgers until 1918. Then he was traded to the Pittsburgh Pirates. Casey loved playing jokes, and the fans loved his _____. When Casey returned to his old stadium for the first time as a Pirate, he planned a special prank for his old fans. When the announcer called out his name, Casey jogged onto the field to tip his cap to the crowd. As he did, a canary hidden in his cap flew out. The crowd welcomed Casey back with loud _____.

Word List
- antics
- applause
- released
- scheme
- spunky
- suspended

Think About It! What does the article suggest about Casey Stengel?

Name _____ Date _____

Long Life

Read this article to get some tips on how to live a long and healthy life. Use the word list to fill in the blanks.

Dottie Jones recently celebrated her 100th birthday. What made the event even more unusual is that two of her guests were over 100 years old. They say that part of their secret is to keep up their social lives. Here are some other tips that are helping more and more people live to be _____.

If you want to live past 100, you have to take good care of yourself. That means eating _____, exercising your body and your mind, and staying involved with family and friends.

Here are some tips for living a long and healthy life.

Word List

benefits

centenarians

cope

mentally

sensibly

- **Eat Well.** A healthy diet includes lots of vegetables, fruit, protein, and grains.

- **Get Moving!** Exercise offers many _____, including better sleep, better memory, and better health.

- **Chill Out!** People who live longer generally know how to _____ with stress.

- **Keep Learning.** Staying _____ active also leads to a longer, healthier life.

Think About It!

In 1700, the average person lived to be 35. Today the average American lives to be over 80 years old. What do you think has led people to live longer lives?

Name _____ Date _____

Kids Help Pass Safety Laws

How can kids save lives? Fill in the blanks in this article to find out about one kid who made a difference.

When Sean Aiken bought a bike helmet, he never

_____ it would help him so soon.

Only a week later, it saved his life. He was hit by a car while

riding home from school in Tucson, Arizona. Although

his bicycle didn't survive the crash, Sean did. His helmet

_____ him from severe head injuries.

"I used to think helmets were _____.

I thought I would never get hurt," said Sean. "But injuries can and will

happen to you if you're not careful."

Sean later spoke before the Tucson City Council about the

need for bike-helmet _____. This led to

a new Arizona law making it _____ for

_____ to wear helmets while cycling. Now, new

laws like the bike-helmet law Sean Aiken helped pass are saving lives.

Word List

imagined
legislation
mandatory
minors
protected
unnecessary

Think About It!   How do helmet laws save lives?

Name _____ Date _____

The Perfect Pet

Do snakes scare you? Fill in the blanks in this story to read about one girl who loves them.

Word List

badgered
candidates
demonstrated
department
winced

"Why not a cat or a dog...or even a hamster?" Carolyn's mom asked.

"Because they aren't as magnificent as snakes," Carolyn replied. Her mother sighed. Carolyn always had to be different! But Carolyn had _____ her mother relentlessly for months...so off to Perfect Pets they went. Carolyn made a beeline to the reptile _____, where she'd already scoped out some _____.

"I'd like to see this Royal Python," Carolyn requested, indicating a spectacular cinnamon-colored specimen.

Carolyn's mom _____ as the clerk reached into the aquarium. "It's not poisonous, is it?"

"No," the man reassured her. "This python is a real sweetheart...but you do want to handle him carefully." He _____, and then offered to let Carolyn hold the python. She grasped the snake gently but firmly below the head and above the tail. "Do you want a turn?" she offered her mom.

"Absolutely not! Are you sure you wouldn't prefer a gerbil?"

"Positive," said Carolyn. "Cinnamon will make the perfect pet!"

Think About It!   Find one fact about pythons in the story. Then find an opinion.

Name _____ Date _____

Presidential Pets

The White House is a stately place, but it has been home to many pets— who don't always follow presidential etiquette! Fill in the blanks to find out more about pets in the White House.

The White House is usually a serious place. Leaders of other countries bring important _____ to the President. Senators give and receive advice. The President signs bills into law.

However, some presidential pets have turned the White House into a wild and crazy place! President Obama got his family a new pet, Bo, as part of a _____ he made during his election _____.
Bo _____ chewed up the President's gym shoes!

Other presidents have had more unusual pets. John Quincy Adams once kept an alligator. Calvin Coolidge had two _____, a donkey, and a bobcat.

Teddy Roosevelt loved animals and proved it when he moved into the White House in 1901. His six children, plus snakes, rats, and a badger joined him. William Henry Harrison kept a goat and a cow. Woodrow Wilson had a flock of sheep. Thomas Jefferson owned a pair of grizzly bears!

Word List

business
campaign
promise
promptly
raccoons

Think About It!

Why do pets make the White House a more interesting place?

40

Name _____ Date _____

Knuckle Cracking

Some people cringe when they hear the "crack!" of others popping their knuckles. Fill in the blanks to find out what really goes on inside those cracking joints.

_____ to popular belief, cracking

your knuckles doesn't _____ your

joints, _____ to Dr. Thomas

Trumble. He's a professor and surgeon at the University of

Washington's _____ of hand and

microvascular surgery in Seattle, Washington.

　Dr. Trumble _____ cracking

your knuckles to "pulling a suction cup off a window." You

don't harm the window or the suction cup at all. But you do

hear a loud pop. The same is true for knuckles.

　"All joints have a normal _____

of air that helps them move smoothly," Dr. Trumble says.

"When you crack your knuckles, you're just breaking that seal,

so it doesn't do any harm at all. In fact, it feels good."

Word List

- according
- contrary
- damage
- division
- likens
- vacuum

Think About It!

Which of these statements is a fact, and which is an opinion?

Cracking your knuckles does no harm to them.
Cracking your knuckles feels good.

Name _____ Date _____

Why Penguins Wear Tuxedos

Have you ever noticed that penguins look like funny little men in tuxedos? Fill in the blanks to find out how their distinctive look may help keep them safe.

Walking around on two legs with their arms flapping around,

penguins are a _____ and adorable

sight. But how did they get their special look?

Most _____ of penguin

developed a similar color pattern. They have black or dark blue

feathers on their backs and white feathers on their chests and

_____.

Scientists think that this basic pattern _____

because it protected penguins so well from their enemies, such as seals,

in the water. From below, its white chest and stomach hide a penguin in

the glare of _____. From above, its dark back

makes a penguin hard to see against the darkness of the water.

Word List

comical

evolved

species

stomachs

sunlight

Think About It!

Why do scientists think that penguin species developed a similar color pattern?

Name _____ Date _____

Endurance

Can you imagine being trapped on a ship for nine months? Fill in the blanks to learn about one adventurer who survived that fate.

Sir Ernest Shackleton was leading a crew on an

_____ to reach Antarctica.

On January 18, 1915, their ship, the *Endurance*, became trapped

in polar ice. For nine months they waited for the ice to break up.

Finally, in October, the crew abandoned the ship and set sail in

three _____ lifeboats.

Hundreds of miles later, the men reached Elephant Island,

a remote, _____ place. Shackleton

realized that they could not survive there. So, he and five other men

set out in one of the lifeboats for an 800-mile journey to South Georgia

Island. They knew that there were people there who could help them.

Seventeen days later, the men arrived. Shackleton took a ship

back to Elephant Island and rescued the rest of his crew.

_____, everyone was still alive.

After over a year of cold, frostbite, and _____,

the men from the *Endurance* were safe at last.

Word List
amazingly
barren
expedition
rickety
starvation

Think About It!

What happened after Shackleton arrived at South Georgia Island?

Name _____ Date _____

Here Comes the... Maildog?

You may have heard that a dog is a person's best friend. Fill in the blanks to read about a helpful dog from the 1800s.

For three years, from 1883 to 1886, the town of Calico,

California, had a very unusual mail carrier—a dog named Dorsey.

Dorsey was the pet of the town's _____,

Jim Stacy. He went along on Stacy's rounds with him. When Stacy

fell ill and was unable to deliver the mail, he counted on Dorsey

to take over. Stacy made a special _____

for Dorsey and attached a pair of saddlebags to it. Then

he sent Dorsey off with a note tied to his collar. The note

_____ that people place any return

mail in the saddlebags. Dorsey completed his rounds successfully.

When Stacey _____, Dorsey didn't

retire. Instead, he was _____ with his own

_____ mail route.

Word List

harness
official
postmaster
recovered
requested
rewarded

Think About It! How did Dorsey help Jim Stacy? What special tools did Stacy create to allow Dorsey to help?

Old Bones

What unusual discoveries have scientists made about animals that lived long ago? Fill in the blanks in this article to find out.

Ten million years ago, a group of animals gathered at a watering hole in Nebraska. Barrel-bodied _____, 15-foot camels, and other creatures came to drink. Then a volcano _____ 1,000 miles away. Wind carried the volcanic ash great distances. The ash rained down over the animals and buried them.

Dr. Michael Voorhies grew up in Nebraska. As a boy, in 1971, a strange thing happened. He found a baby rhino skull in Nebraska. He dug around it. It was still attached to a skeleton. He kept digging and found five more rhino skeletons.

So far, _____ scientists have found more than 240 complete animal skeletons in that area. They even discovered the remains of a tiny three-toed horse.

Finding so many skeletons in one place is very unusual. Usually bones are _____ far apart by wind, waves, or animals. But these remains were _____ exactly where they were by the volcanic ash that buried them.

Word List

- erupted
- fossil
- preserved
- rhinoceroses
- scattered

Think About It! Why was the discovery of the Nebraska animal bones so important?

Name _____ Date _____

What's the Word?

Have you ever made up a new word? Americans invent many new words. Fill in the blanks in this article to find out how it happens.

Next time you eat potato chips in the bathtub during a blizzard, think about this: *potato chips*, *bathtub*, and *blizzard* are all words that were born in the U.S.A.!

Americans have added thousands of words to the English _____. "These words make up the story of America," says Allan Metcalf, who studies language. "They show our changing _____ over time."

The word *carpool* was invented in 1962. Around that time, Americans were becoming more aware of the _____. To help protect the air, people began to share, or "pool" car rides.

Eighty years ago, there was no such thing as a "teenager." Until the early 1900s, kids age 13 or 14 were viewed as adults. At that age, many kids ended their schooling and went to work. But new _____, which ended child labor, required kids to finish high school. People in their teens were no longer children, but they weren't yet adults. So *teenager* was the perfect word to give these 13- to 19-year-olds an _____.

Word List

attitudes
dictionary
environment
identity
regulations

Think About It! How does the invention of new words show changing attitudes over time?

Name _____   Date _____

Endangered Animals

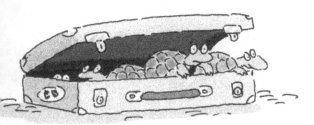

Endangered animals are at risk of dying out completely, so there are laws to protect them. Fill in the blanks to read how some people try to get around those laws.

Endangered animals are big business among some pet sellers. It's illegal to import or sell endangered animals in the United States. But some people try to get them in just the same. Here are a few _____ endangered pet stories.

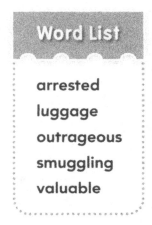

Word List

arrested
luggage
outrageous
smuggling
valuable

● Guess what officials in Sweden found inside a woman's blouse? Live baby grass snakes—65 of them! The woman planned to start a reptile farm. Instead, she was _____ for _____!

● Imagine someone bringing a sackful of endangered tortoises onboard a plane—as carry-on _____. The baggage was labeled "coconuts." This trick worked until the "coconuts" started to crawl inside the bag!

● One man wore a very _____ piece of clothing. A padded vest hid 40 eggs of Australia's endangered black palm cockatoo—one of the smartest parrots on Earth. The eggs were worth at least $10,000 each. That's a $400,000 vest!

Think About It!   What are some animals people have tried to smuggle?

Answer Key

These word lists show
the correct order of the
words that complete
each cloze passage.

Passage 1: pointless, distracted, considering, imprisoned, flaw

Passage 2: claimed, disagreeing, wrapped, unbuttoned, gentleness

Passage 3: astonished, lunchroom, recently, genuinely, momentarily

Passage 4: invitation, captured, tacky, anxious, received

Passage 5: neighbor, chuckled, scissors, tumbled, success

Passage 6: nightshirt, wildly, guard, investigate, thief

Passage 7: assignment, signifies, grumbled, excellent, swoop

Passage 8: pressure, gorilla, weightless, peaceful, vivid

Passage 9: appealing, durable, unusual, designs, coverings

Passage 10: assortment, jewels, expert, target, flick, propel

Passage 11: signal, bandannas, bandages, chaps, brush

Passage 12: continually, irritate, guaranteed, confronted, startled

Passage 13: avoid, naturally, significantly, influences, nervous, surrounding

Passage 14: famous, powdered, overnight, creation, patented

Passage 15: participate, discovered, abilities, activities, gymnastics

Passage 16: granted, vast, foolish, scolded, pity

Passage 17: arid, parachute, confine, overhead, smother, appear

Passage 18: sundaes, marshmallow, apricot, tortilla, resemble

Passage 19: dazzling, toiletries, boomerangs, fashionable, entertainment

Passage 20: enormous, suspect, voyage, unsinkable, hull

Passage 21: similar, newborn, rodents, chief, hibernate

Passage 22: liquid, trudging, steamy, local, infections

Passage 23: doubt, consume, expect, vanilla, popularity

Passage 24: version, professional, attend, prevalent, support

Passage 25: howling, supplies, temperatures, canyons, summit

Passage 26: northward, possibility, hauled, diseases, drained, shortcut

Passage 27: decorate, quality, insulation, oxygen, chemical

Passage 28 : spectacle, schedule, unpredictable, performance, reliability

Passage 29: spunky, released, suspended, scheme, antics, applause

Passage 30: centenarians, sensibly, benefits, cope, mentally

Passage 31: imagined, protected, unnecessary, legislation, mandatory, minors

Passage 32: badgered, department, candidates, winced, demonstrated

Passage 33: business, promise, campaign, promptly, raccoons

Passage 34: contrary, damage, according, division, likens, vacuum

Passage 35: comical, species, stomachs, evolved, sunlight

Passage 36: expedition, rickety, barren, amazingly, starvation

Passage 37: postmaster, harness, requested, recovered, rewarded, official

Passage 38: rhinoceroses, erupted, fossil, scattered, preserved

Passage 39: dictionary, attitudes, environment, regulations, identity

Passage 40: outrageous, arrested, smuggling, luggage, valuable

Quick Cloze Passages for Boosting Comprehension: Grades 4–6 © 2012 by Scholastic Teaching Resources

Printed in the USA
CPSIA information can be obtained
at www.ICGtesting.com
LVHW071126100124
768241LV00080B/3115

9 780545 301107